# Hands That Br

Sundress Publications • Knoxville, TN

ISBN: 978-1-939675-58-3
Library of Congress: 2017950246
Published by Sundress Publications
www.sundresspublications.com

Editor: Erin Elizabeth Smith
Editorial Assistant: Jane Huffman

Special thanks to Danielle Alexander.


Colophon: This book is set in Adobe Caslon Pro.

Cover Image: "Self Love" by Aydee Lopez Martinez

Cover Design: Kristen Ton

Author Photo: Most Exalted

Book Design: Erin Elizabeth Smith

# Hands That Break & Scar
## Sarah A. Chavez

# ACKNOWLEDGMENTS

Grateful acknowledgments made to the following publications where some of these poems first appeared:

*American Life in Poetry*: "In Childhood"

*The Battered Suitcase*: "When the Heat Ends"

*Bent Pin Quarterly*: "Running into Things"

*Blood Lotus*: "When She Asked Was I Afraid of Needles"

*CALYX, A Journal of Art and Literature by Women*: "How Waitresses Walk Home," "Grandma's Hands" (under the title "About Grandma's Hand"), and "She Came Home Crying Again"

*The Fourth River*: "Viscosity"

*Green Hills Literary Lantern*: "When the Woodward Park Attendant Offered You the Handicap Rate"

*North American Review*: "Tag"

*Not Somewhere Else But Here: A Contemporary Anthology of Women and Place* (Sundress Publications): "The Mexican American Parade"

*Political Punch: Contemporary Poems on the Politics of Identity* (Sundress Publications): "Neighborhood Watch" and "Praise This Land, The San Joaquin Valley"

*So To Speak*: "This, Like So Much"

*Spoon River Poetry Review*: "Thirteen and Catholic"

*Stirring: A Literary Collection*: "The Day the Alligators Feasted on Time"

*Stone's Throw Magazine*: "What We Didn't Want"

*Weber – The Contemporary West*: "Full Again"

*Women Arts Quarterly*: "The Good, The Bad, & The Ugly" (under the title "Watching *The Good, The Bad & The Ugly* with My Dad")

A version of "Another Epistle" appears in the chapbook, *All Day, Talking* (dancing girl press, 2014).

# TABLE OF CONTENTS

## I

## II

## III

# I

"...there's no-
thing more you can chop off    or graft on me that
will change my soul.    I remain who I am, multiple
and one."

- Gloria Anzaldúa

# The Mexican-American Parade

Used to happen downtown every year.
Fresno closed off the streets from Tuolumne and "M"
south to Tulare and west to Van Ness.
My dad took me and my light-skinned sister
to watch the floats decorated with red and white
roses tucked into green foliage. The high school
band marched while the auxiliary team
kicked their dark legs and threw
their batons between the flowered floats.
We ate street tacos and churros, drank Horchata,
while people who looked more like my dad
than me walked around, rolling their Rs,
muttering, *Está tan caliente.*

The only women caught wearing blousy
peasant shirts and full skirts trimmed at the base
with colorful ribbons were the girls dancing
the *baile folklorico* at the end of the parade route
on a small wooden stage, where the rhythmic, hollow
sound of their *zapateadas* could be heard
for blocks. Afterward, those girls took off
the costumes of their mothers, put their jeans
and bodysuits back on, teased out their gelled bangs,
and slid on dark lipstick before joining the crowd.
I begged my dad to buy us a souvenir before returning
us to our mother's. Beside one of the vendors,
he held a t-shirt flat against my shoulders.

When I looked down, I could see two eagles, their claws
clutching fast to flags—one red, white and green,
the other red, white and blue. Their beaks almost touched,
mirror images of one another,
reflections across water, across a border.
The corners of the flags both dripped red,
bled into a pool beneath their talons, filling
the lower white space of the shirt. *Esto es usted*,
he said to me, pointing at the red pool
*y usted debería estar orgulloso*.

# Heredity

Some relatives say
I look like mom—
cupid bow lips, large teeth.
Other relatives say
I look like dad—
thick fleshy lobes at the end
of long ears. They say
I have her hair, straight
and long, but darker.
And others say
I have his hands, muscular
and square, only smaller.
Her height, his dark skin.
His father's father's hazel eyes,
her mother's mother's shrewd sense
of humor. Her brother's
ability to draw, his brother's
capacity for Jose Cuervo. My dad's
mom's legs, my mom's dad's
suspicious brow. My mom's bust,
my dad's cheek bones,
my mom's sharp chin and my dad's
penchant for weight
around the middle.
The only thing left
to claim for myself
is this vigilant tongue.

## What We Didn't Want

I don't know how other people kill bugs, but my family used fire.
The first time my mom let me help, she handed me
the can of Aqua Net while holding the lighter
in front of the wasp's nest that hung from the porch light
over our front door. *When I flick the flint, point at the nest*
*and push down.* The hiss of the hairspray through flame
and the crackling of their papery wings was a song.
*Now, don't ever do that without me,* she said.

The next day, Tracy from across the street and I went
searching for things to burn.  She borrowed her mom's hairspray,
I stole a lighter from 7-11, and we tested our blow torch
on everything: newspaper, candy, grass, wet leaves, dry leaves, the mean
neighbor lady's roses, my little sister's Barbies, plastic bags, the terrible
Yorkie sweater Grandma Shannon gave me for Christmas, the note
listing chores, family photos of fathers not really in the picture.

It was so easy to get rid of what we didn't want, and afterwards
the smell of lighter fluid clung to our hair like perfume.

## Constructing Childhood

Christy and I played in the dumpster across the street
from Pickett & Sons Construction. It was best when we found bricks.
Bricks were useful. We dragged them to our empty backyard
and stacked them in the shape of a room. For months,
we collected bricks, one on top of another. When the walls reached
as high as my younger sister's head, we both laid down
in the middle of our creation. We watched the cycle of the sun,
gazed at the stars, held hands, and felt at home.

# Viscosity

*It was good for the skin to touch the Earth . . . the soil was soothing, strengthening, cleansing and healing.*
—Luther Standing Bear


None of us are allowed to go
outside barefoot because glass shards
from busted car windows, smoldering
cigarette butts, and cracked hypodermic needles
litter the streets in our neighborhood.
We can't help ourselves, though—
there is something delicious
about the bottoms of our feet
forming to the bumpy surface of the asphalt—
always warm, except in the depths of summer,
when it is searing. Once the sun
is directly overhead, like the yellow orb
in our coloring books, we dance
restlessly on the white concrete
of someone's mother's carport,
pairs of naked feet in various stages of tan
and burn. We dare each other
to walk slowly across the glistening black
of Dakota Avenue with no shoes,
to see who can withstand
heat the longest.

This Saturday Tracy, Bobby, Evelyn, and Ryan dare me,
pushing and clucking like chickens.

Halfway across the street, it burns
like stovetop coils. Running
is for sissies, and it's too far to turn back. I'm afraid
to look weak, as the other kids yell
and crack their dirty hands.
I clench shut my eyes to stop the tears,
and as the skin on my soles begins bonding
to the street, the heat eases.
Something wants me to cross.
It's as if the living rocks, aggregate and slag,
melted and rolled thin,
still have connection, can feel desperation
alive in my veins as I make way
to the other side.

# Temptation

Sunday afternoon,
my little sister and I
in spring church dresses,
white ruffled socks, black
patent leather shoes
traipsed about
Abuelita's back yard.
We were told
not to touch anything
in the garden. We kept
ourselves from the aloe,
the lemon grass
boiled into tea
for stomach aches;
the tomatoes and parsley;
denied the green onions,
whose long skinny fingers
curled invitation.
But the pomegranates,
giant and round
as Christmas bulbs,
such soft red skin
like the tender give
and gift of a bruise
were too much—
their little upside down
crowns, like open mouths

calling to us.
I twisted one
from the flimsy branch,
but it was Christy
who stuck her stubby finger
into the mouth,
ripping open the skin,
the red beads of fruit
flying out, bursting
in our hands
like tiny bombs of blood.

# The Day the Alligators Feasted on Time

Time was as fluid as water,
and like water on the asphalt,
it evaporated before we could look,
look away, and look back.

And yet it held importance
in worlds we did not honor,
but we honored each other's presence
and without adherence

to the arbitrary rules of adults,
the tangibility of each other's hands
would have to wait until
a week of grounding was over.

Tracy learned at her school,
that a minute consisted
of sixty seconds, and a second
could be measured

through alligators. *One alligator,*
*two alligator. Like that*, she said.
We checked the clock again,
saw we had only three minutes

before I had to go home.
But what can be done

in three minutes, except watch
the time slip past?

Not wanting to part early, we sat
on the steps of her mother's porch,
decided to count alligators.
We did the math. It broke down

to one hundred and eighty alligators.
*One alligator, two alligator,*
*three alligator, four alligator,*
*five alligator, six . . .*

The four syllables of alligator
were rhythmic, became hypnotic.
Our warm bodies swayed, shoulder against
shoulder, and our fingers danced

on the other's knee for every number
until the gators became
overpowering. Filled with the humming
vibrations of time, we leapt

to our feet and stomped for every last
syllable. *Sixteen al-li-ga-TOR,*
*seventeen al-li-ga-TOR, eighteen*
*al-li-ga-TOR . . .* The weak beams

of the porch quaked under
the devastating weight

of our small feet. And this,
like all things we did together,

became transcendent.
We didn't stop at alligator one
hundred and eighty. I never
went home. We just kept stomping

and counting, our arms linked, the alligators
piling higher and higher, rising with the moon.

# II

"The day is like us, she thinks; it hasn't decided what to become."

- Philip Levine

# When She Asked Was I Afraid of Needles

I looked down at my hand, then straight ahead,
raised my eyebrows high and said, *Hell no.*

At recess, we cracked the plastic case of the pen
against the metal bracing of the jungle gym

and buried it in the sand below, where classmates
planted marbles, rubber balls, love notes.

With a pocket knife I'd hidden in my shoe, Eren cut
the tube of ink at a diagonal. I blocked her

from the teachers standing near the swing-set
by the monkey-bars, where they leaned against

the kickball wall and drank coffee, pretending
to watch out for injury or mischief. She pulled

the lighter from her school-issued pants pocket
and showed me how she had stitched the needle

along the inside seam of her polo. *My brother told me
we won't get an infection if we sterilize it,* she said, guiding

the tiny flame, letting it lick the needle up and down
until it was too hot to hold. I'd seen her brother

in my neighborhood, tattoos covering his body
like small paintings, the edges raised like Braille

if you closed your eyes and touched. Once he was nice,
gave me a ride home in his white, lowered El Camino.

That day, I didn't have to run past the apartments
where the men would leer and grab

their dicks through their pants and yell,
*Come here, baby, I've got something for you.*

In his car, I felt strong and safe sitting up
in the leather seats, so the neighborhood people

could see me through the window
above the clean, shining door.

*I'll go first*, I said, spreading my thumb
and pointer finger to flatten the web

of my hand. *Now, we'll be hermanas,* she said
and kissed me on the cheek before dragging

the needle across my outstretched skin.

# Tag

The kids run in circles around the play yard—
their blue uniform pant legs pumping rhythmically,
their skinny arms outstretched, fingers splayed

to catch the shoulder of anyone they can. Nicole tags
Nick and yells *Pork 'n Beans* 'cause he's Portuguese.
All the kids run circles around the play yard.

I dodge Nick until he grabs my dark arm
and hollers *Mess in a Can* 'cause I'm Mexican.
Now their skinny arms are outstretched, fingers splayed,

grasping at the air to pull them faster along.
I spin around, smack Shannon, shout *Potato Eater*,
while all the other kids run circles around the play yard.

Shannon slaps Joey, cries *Slanty-eyes*, and Joey crashes
into Ben, who's not even playing, and wails *Rag Head*.
Ben outstretches his skinny arms, fingers splayed,

pinches Adam hard and mutters *Fag*, running back
toward the concrete basketball courts. Recess is almost over,
but all the kids still run circles around the play yard
their skinny arms outstretched, their trigger fingers splayed.

# Cousin Conversion at Great Aunt Frances' House

Angelica, with long dark hair in a permed wave across her shoulders,
pulled on the braids that fell from the sides of my head like bell chords

and called me a baby. Lil' Benny swatted the skirt of my ruffled dress,
echoing Angelica's verdict. I tried not to cry.

*She doesn't know any better*, Franny said. *You know
her mom's white.* Franny—though she was only a few years older—

had two holes in each ear lobe, wore stone-washed jeans
and eyeliner. Ringed fingers wrapped around my arm

as she dragged me past the dining room where my dad sat speaking Spanish
with all his brothers, distant relatives, and neighbors, who gathered

every year around the grown-up table to drink Budweisers and wine.
In the guest room, she dug into drawers, finding jeans and a black sweater.

*Put these on*, she commanded, pulling the rubber bands
off the ends of my braids. I stepped out of the dress, pushing it

under the bed with my foot as I pulled on the jeans. Franny fluffed
my hair with her fingertips, nodding. I moved to the mirror

above the dresser where the cousins' school portraits were tucked
into the corner alongside pictures of Uncle Benny and Aunt Francis

at their anniversary, and someone's graduation party,
where the family sat crowded on the couch, looking comfortable,

smiling. I gazed at my image framed by all their brown faces looking
past me, joy crinkling the skin around the corners of all their striking eyes.

## The Good, The Bad, and The Ugly

Late afternoon sun shines
through the tan and white striped curtains,
creating spots of light
across the brown carpet.
On the old console television,
Clint Eastwood as Blondie
wears an embroidered serape, holds
a gun to Tuco's head.
They are locked
in a timeless battle
of hatred and necessity,
the type of battle
that is always about money.

I point to the screen
and say that Tuco looks
a lot like Uncle Emanuel.
*That's the ugly*, my dad smirks—
my first lesson in understanding
that even in our house,
Blondie is always the good one.

# Running into Things

It was my uncle's M.O. to drive drunk
into buildings, especially homes
where family and friends lived.
At ten, I was afraid of earthquakes
and woke one night to a tenuous shaking.
I grabbed my sister and searched
for our mother, who was outside, trying
to convince my uncle to stop ramming
the sad metal siding-skirt of our mobile home.
Since then, he has kept himself busy
punching through garage doors
and mowing over shade bushes.

It wasn't until a decade later that he hit
his own place. That Tuesday afternoon
when the Motel 6 manager felt the quake,
knowing it was no aftershock, he slipped
on his house shoes and stumbled
outside. The long nose of my uncle's '73
gold-tinted Impala was burrowed deep
into a corner of cement, just around
the north side from the main office.
This was no normal act of carelessness, no
run-of-the-mill slip of the foot
on the gas. To jump the concrete
parking barrier, the standard thirteen-inch
curb, and another four feet of sidewalk,

to puncture a foot of cement, metal supports
and all reeked of intention.
My uncle stepped out of the car,
rubbed his gin-bleary eyes, wiped blood
from his brow, and proceeded
to his second-story room.

When the police knocked, he opened the door,
a stiff glass of Seagram's in hand, and invited
them inside. It didn't occur to him
they'd come to arrest him. He'd done nothing
he hadn't been doing for thirty years.
He told the manager, like he had my mother
back when I was ten, he knew a guy;
it would only take a couple
hundred bucks to fill the hole.

# This, Like So Much

On the night of my first kiss,
I was supposed to have been home
by 10 p.m., but we just kept walking,
our fingers interlaced, talking about
Clive Barker books. When we got
to my front door, the porch light
was out, and I thought it lucky,
because this time, I'd remembered
to leave my retainer at home
just in case.

We stood in the half dark, the glow
from the street lamp back-lighting
his silhouette. He brushed his fingers
down my cheek, while his other hand
slid under my hair. We were smart
enough not to talk. He merely bent
down and touched his lips to mine—
sweetly—at first. My body both burned
and relaxed, my mind for once not racing.

I went in the house, feeling dizzy,
giddy, sat on the couch and tried
to keep the feeling, tuck it away
where I could always come back to find it,
but from the other room I could hear
my mom's shrill screaming, her boyfriend

pleading. The small mobile home shook
as he tried to slam the bedroom door
in her face, but she followed him,
pushing at his back, yanking his shirt,
yelling all the while, *Don't you
walk away from me*! They brushed
past me, out the front door,
and into the cool night air I had just left.

After the screech of his tires faded
down the block, my mom stomped back
into the house, her face twisted in anger.
The fair skin of her neck blazed
as she grabbed a glass from the table.
The sweet, high ting echoed
in the shower of shining shards
that bloomed from the newly formed
hollow in the living room wall:
no moment of happiness without cost.

# Summer Rides

The Four Seasons' security guard,
who didn't guard much of anything,
let us ride on the golf cart
that putted nightly
through the mobile home park.

He leered at Tracy's budding body
on the seat next to him while I gazed
at the stars from the bench in back,
memorizing the feel of midnight
breeze on my face.

*I see you reading those paperbacks*
*on your porch*, he said to me
on our second revolution around the park.
*What you reading that crap for?*
And with the full sincerity
of my twelve years I said,
*Because it's romantic.*
Looking over his shoulder,
he laughed. *Is that so?*

For another twenty minutes,
we put-putted quietly past
darkened windows, past
busted street lights and sleeping
chained dogs, until the close

of his shift when he stopped
at the edge of the block
between our homes.
*Alright girls, end of the line.*

# III

"...we flew
into a world that kicked
our hearts so hard with its beauty
it always left a bruise."
- David Hernandez

# Thirteen and Catholic

Even though my mom and the priests say it's a sin,
I let the neighbor boy run his hands over the front
of my shirt. Tracy did it with Bobby, and she says it feels

so much better than when you do it yourself,
and it's not creepy like when the doctor does it.
I think about how Jesus can see everything you do,

even when you're in the bathroom, my grandma says—
and how He must certainly see me now. As my nipples
harden and warmth begins to bloom between my thighs,

I try to remember if this is a mortal or venial sin, and can't,
so I guess it must not be mortal, but it's possible that under
the clothes is, so I stop his hand as it begins to slide beneath

my volleyball jersey. Voice deep and soft in my ear telling me
it's okay, his breath is like a warm breeze, something Fresno
hasn't had in weeks, and it buckles my knees in surrender.

# Doing Laundry

Tracy stood in the frame of the side door
and watched me load colors into the Maytag.
I pointed the knob to cold, making sure
I didn't shrink anything again, measured

the grainy detergent with the scoop that hung
on a nail beside the shelf above the machine.
Tracy was wearing cut-off jean shorts and a tank top,
her new bra showing in the deep dip of the armhole,

the subtle swell of pre-adolescent breasts
pressed against the thin cotton fabric.
Her knees made me understand the term
"knock-kneed," the uneven bones like apples

jammed between pretzel sticks. My parents'
friends told me I have nice legs. *Gams*, Candy said
when I brought mom's lunch to her at work,
*good, tan solid gams.* Our bodies had begun to change.

While Tracy "blossomed" I just got bigger everywhere.
The school nurse had sent a note home that said
even fat girls needed bras and the boys
were making comments behind my back.

Tracy and I were the first girls in our class to wear
real bras with adjustable straps and back clasps,
and that meant we got the sex talk. We watched
the video where a priest explained that breasts led

to sex with boys, and sex was a sin God punished
with pregnancy. My cousin Angelica got pregnant
when she was fourteen, and her feet swelled so big
she couldn't wear her Adidas anymore. She cried

and swore the day she went into labor, the neighbors
all coming out of their homes to watch her toddle,
barefoot, out of her boyfriend's mom's house
so my grandfather could drive her to the hospital.

All the cousins were forced to visit her in the maternity ward,
the wrinkled purple heads of the newborns like soggy raisins.
There was so much crying—the mothers, the babies,
my grandmother, making the sign of the cross

over and over again, twice for everyone. Angelica
came home three days later, her body stretched and older.
She couldn't do anything or go anywhere. Instead of cruising
Blackstone in her boyfriend's truck on Friday nights

or smoking *mota* behind the grade school backstop
like they used to, she sat home breastfeeding and folding
the baby's small clothes into the emptied dresser drawer
in the room that was no longer just hers.

*You're super good at that*, Tracy said, as I put one article
of clothing in at a time, so they wouldn't bunch and twist
together in the machine. *It's not hard*, I said, lowering the lid.
*Yeah, but you're good at all this*, she said, sweeping

her arm to indicate the laundry room and bathroom,
the kitchen where earlier I'd made my little sister's lunch,
the vacuum resting against the wall in the hallway
among stray Barbies, crayons, and barrettes.

*You'll make a good mom*, she said, as if cleaning
was all you had to know, or maybe because most days
I stayed home, did as I was told. *I'm never going to be a mother*, I said,
knowing neither she, nor anyone else, would believe me.

## The Language of Stories

When freckle-faced, red-haired Kellie comes over
to my house in the summer, we watch T.V.
below the rotating ceiling fan, our stomachs flat
on the carpet, close enough to change channels

on the console. We flip past Matlock, People's Court,
and infomercials featuring Miss Cleo's psychic call-ins,
old ladies saved by Life Alert, until we get to *Telemundo*,
the channel my sister and I watched at our grandmother's.
There, at her house in Merced, we helped her
make *chile verde* while the six-inch black and white
in the corner played *Imperio De Cristal.*

Grandma blamed it on the onions, but in between chops,
she would glance up at the screen, react to the distress
on the smooth, auburn faces and lean over the cutting board,
wrinkled cheeks peppered with tears.

This is the show on now, and Kellie wants to know
what they are saying. My grandmother isn't here to translate
and my dad is at his house and it is just us two girls, alone
at my mom's, where only English is spoken, but Spanish
is my language too, and I know that I am supposed to know.

My grandma spent that week pointing at items in her house,
telling us the right word. We repeated the rolled R's
and inverted sentence structure, but none of that comes to me now

while Kellie looks at my mouth as if my tongue
should have this language hardwired in. So, I pretend
to understand the molten sounds emitting from those women
with colorful lips who talk so much faster than my family.

Jumping to my feet, I make up the whole plot. In a voice
pinched high, I point to the screen and tell Kellie about the love affair
between Maria and Guillermo, about their love child, and Reynaldo,
the horrible boss man who is trying to come between them,
and Sylvia's death, and Juan's reunion with an unknown twin.

Kellie's blue eyes light up. She says this is her favorite
soap opera now too and wonders how anyone
can make this stuff up, but I think I understand, because
the only words I recognized—*beso*, *abrazo*, *amor* and *familia*–
are all anyone needs for a good story.

# Real Mexicans Know How to Dance

*You dunno how to dance!*
Angelica laughed as she elbowed Franny,
who laughed too. Benny shrugged,
grabbed the remote and flopped
onto the couch, *Me neither.*
*We'll teach you*, Angelica offered,
signaling Franny with the point of her chin.

For hours, we watched videos
of Bobby Brown, C & C Music Factory,
Salt n' Peppa, and MC Hammer. During commercials,
we mimicked the slightly dressed women,
pumping our arms and legs,
elbows bent like ineffectual wings, flapping
grossly, a step out of time with the music. We practiced
bending our knees and shuffling side to side
like a football drill. We kicked and dropped, spun,
pushed out our chests and shook our hips
and adolescent asses. *You got it,*
Angelica sang, nodding toward me.
Lil' Benny snapped his fingers and rolled
his shoulders while CeCe Peniston sang,
*Finally, it has happened to me right in front*
*of my face and I just cannot hide it.*
Franny grabbed my hands
and we fake cha-cha-ed, cheeks close
like the old Mexican couples at the VFW dances.

Our grandmother and Nina heard us,
came to see the commotion, and stood
in the doorway. When we stopped flailing,
they clapped and whistled, and Angelica
and Franny took bows, grabbed me
and my sister's hands, made us do the same.

# Only You, Little Sister

I remember the time you got hurt,
your bike rocketing down
the steep, grassy slope
that slid into the baseball field
that flooded
whenever it rained.

Everyone before you
jostled as the tires
of their bikes hit
grass clumps and small
pebbles on the green
and uneven ground.

You went down last.
All the neighborhood kids
leaned on their handlebars
and called to you, chanting
your name, coaxing you.
You didn't square your feet
on the pedals, your hands
too loose on the bars.

You hit the dip
that no one else hit,
and your body tumbled
over the handles, knees

hitting the ground hard,
grass staining the new rip
in the leg of your pants.

With your body tangled
in the aluminum of the bike frame,
eyes wide as Coke can tops,
you looked up to me
as if to say it was my fault
the ground didn't soften
for your impact.

# In the Pool

Christy and I spent most of our summer days and nights there.
When the sun was up and the neighborhood children gathered,
kicking and splashing, we'd deafen their noise to a low rumble
by submerging our heads. Hair floated around our faces
like underwater clouds. Our mouths moved. We pretended to talk
and understand each other in the dense, chlorinated water.

Together, we'd dare the other kids to swim by the big vents,
the ones that were said to suck in little girls' hair and drown them
before a lifeguard even knew what happened.
At least that was the story, but we knew it wasn't true;
we'd tried it once. Between the two of us,
there were miles of hair, and that vent didn't want any of it.

Our favorite time was at night, when the huge lights in the deep end
looked like an oncoming car when we swam toward them.
We'd race, pushing off the shallow-end wall, holding our breath
as long as possible in a game of chicken no one could lose.
When we reached those steady headlights, they were warm
against our hands and we felt triumphant, as if once again
we cheated death, and summers like this would never end.

# When My Sister Came Home Crying Again

I grabbed my baseball bat. The one I use for softball practice in the early afternoons when school let out. It's a good bat, an Easton, metal, with white gripping tape on the handle. I learned to use its heft in the store that day, on my dad's weekend, when he took us to Big 5 Sporting Goods, and the young clerk with brown hair and light eyes kept smiling at me while he showed Christy soccer cleats. My dad actually picked it out, pulled it down from the rack full of so many colors and styles, a virtual metal rainbow. Another man, older, wearing plaid polyester pants, some nosy pervert just hanging around said, *The most important factor to keep in mind, from Little League to the pros, is that buying a bat is a personal decision. This one looks sturdy*, my dad said, holding the bat at the barrel, loose and tentative, reverent—like the way you'd hold the blade of a knife, pointing the grip at me. I held out my hands, wrapped my fingers around it, let the weight of the fat barrel pull on my arms before I reared up my shoulders and swung, accidentally knocking over a plastic display case. Neon green tennis balls flew like radiated birds and bounced all over the store. The young clerk said, *That bat sure could do a lot of damage*. And that's why I grab it now and head out the front door.

Quinceañera

Maria looked like a brown Cinderella
as the jeweled hem of her blue
satin gown skimmed the floor
of the VFW Hall on Belmont.

Between the fold-out tables covered
in butcher paper that her mom had adorned
with candelabra center pieces
from the 98-cent Store, Maria and her procession
walked in the measured steps of a bridal party.
*Practique para luego*, mi abuela once told me.

Behind her, all the boy cousins were crammed
awkwardly into stiff suits, the squeak
from their brand new shoes echoing
off the dingy walls, embarrassing
the girl cousins they escorted.

The florescent lights twinkled,
winking off the diamonds in Maria's tiara
which pretended to hold the mountain of dark curls
sprayed in place on top of her head.

She wore matching heels and make-up,
which we never got to do, though we sometimes
snuck into her older sister's room
and took from the dresser the small cosmetics bag

that had a mirror and red lipstick inside.
One afternoon, her father came home and found us
dancing a counterfeit salsa in the living room,
our lips like small spring roses,
and we thought he was going to get mad and yell,
like he had when we exploded
candy bars in the microwave, but instead
he laughed. *Don't try to grow up too fast,*
*mija,* he said. *My heart couldn't take it.*

# Watching a Fire

The homeless man squatting
in the abandoned house next door
seemed to be building a throne
in the backyard. He placed debris
around him in a circle and sat stately,
straight-backed in the middle
of discarded toilet paper rolls, candy
bar wrappers, crumpled newspapers,
Big Mac clamshells, and empty
glass bottles of Heineken.

He was perfectly calm, lean, and tan,
nascent hair sprouting out the top
of his head like flame grass.
He spoke to invisible subjects,
whose eyes, like haunted mirrors,
reflected something awful.

From the pocket of his jeans,
he pulled a blank match book,
no name or address to hint
at where he'd been. He tore out
a match and slowly dragged the head
across the scratchy strip
on the back of the pack. Tucking
the light between the folds
of yesterday's *Fresno Bee*, the flash

blossomed like an angry tulip.
In the distance, sirens sang.

# IV

"I bare a wound, and dare myself to bleed."
-    Theodore Roethke

# How Waitresses Walk Home in the Dark

Ever since Sandra got mugged
walking to her car after the night shift,
and the assholes took all the tips
she'd earned and her purse and the watch
that used to be her mother's, and left her
with a broken tooth and a shiner
the color of deep space, we've all gone about
preparing ourselves in different ways.

Shelly carries mace
in the right pocket of her apron,
practices while we smoke behind the building
on break—*John Wayne style*
she says, spinning the can on her middle
finger and pointing its puckered mouth
at Jose the dishwasher, who tells her
to knock that shit off.

Norma got a whistle,
one of those police whistles that can blow
out an ear drum if you're too close.
She got it from her cop boyfriend, who comes in
every Wednesday during her shift
for free dinner. *I know what else
she did for that whistle*, Johnny the cook
jokes from behind the grill.

Me though, on my break,
I just work on my fuck-you face,
staring straight and dead-eyed
into the bathroom mirror. I try
to look as if I don't care, as if anything
they do to me doesn't matter.
I act as if I have nothing
to lose. And most days, I don't.

# When the Heat Ends

Dear Carole, do you remember the time
you and I went swimming
in the middle of that lightning storm?
You hoisted me over the fence
so I could jimmy the lock and let you in.
We swam in our clothes as it started raining—
the thick drops like explosions
in the chlorinated water.
Those Central Valley summer storms
just make it hotter, the air heavier
than we thought breathable.

Remember how you used to smoke
and swim at the same time? Even though
I made fun of you—it was fucking impressive.
Using those large breasts as buoys,
you leaned your head back, hair fanned
out across the water, one large, soft arm
sliding lazily across the clear surface,
the other lifting a cigarette
to your smiling lips.

And you know what I was thinking
about the other day? That time I smoked
my first cigarette sitting on the patio
with you at Krakatoa. Our hands
clasped across the table, talking

through the steam of black coffee,
you told me I just wasn't that cool.
Remember how I waited
before reaching over for the pack,
popping out a cigarette
like in the old black-and-white movies
we watched on Sunday afternoons,
and lit up? It makes me laugh
even now, that wide-eyed look of shock
on your face. How proud
you were of how natural it looked
when I sucked in the smoke,
blew it through my nostrils.

Remember the day I left
and how you didn't move
to stop me? The whir of the air conditioner
helpless against the dry heat
that rose in waves off the cement outside
and crept through the apartment
windows like a thief.
Silent, your body, back to the door,
stretched, across
the cushions of that sagging
brown couch we used to share,
leaning against one another
after work in the evenings.
It was as if you thought
if you didn't look, I wouldn't go.
If there was no closure, no good-bye,

no forgiveness, then I'd have to unpack
the truck and lie next to you
on the couch, our skin sticky, fused
by this heat that I wouldn't miss.
You wouldn't remember this,
but in the truck, I cried myself sick,
cried so hard the capillaries
under my eyes burst like sun rays.

It hurt like the times we laughed
stitches into our sides, our breath
cut short,
and we couldn't stop.

# Waiting for the Bus

They think I'm watching them
because they are men
and I am a woman, sitting
on this downtown bench,
my arms and legs exposed
to release the heat that traps itself
even in cotton. They think
I'm watching them
because it's summer, when the days
are long and the nights steamy
and sleepless.

They flex their arms, dark with sun
and dirt, look from beneath their hard hats,
lift tubes, pull over trucks, uncoil
bright orange electrical cords.
I can smell the musk of work
and I'm wanting,
not to be with them, but to *be* them.
Not to touch the muscles
that contract under their shirts,
but to *have* those muscles.

I used to do what they do—
lift and pull, pound the sidewalk
in work-boots and ripped jeans,
wipe dirt and perspiration

from my upper lip with my shirt.
And I'm not romanticizing.
That kind of work beats the body,
makes it submissive
to the passage of time, all the minutes
and hours and days wear down the bones
but clear the mind.

I miss feeling capable, my body
an instrument
of productivity, and my mind
focused, expanding
on the meditation of hammer
on nail, the sledge against concrete,
creating pieces jagged and vibrant
as musical notes. The tremors
of the steel nose against everything
charging the blood.

# When the Woodward Park Attendant Offered You the Handicap Rate
*For Daddio*

Your brown face turned red like the tomatoes you harvested,
and the metal of your brace twinkled like the shine of the machine
that mangled your arm. She smiled kindly enough
while your girlfriend giggled and said, *At least we'll get in at a discount*,
but I could see the tendons taut in the back of your neck.

To be nice and smile, to say *No, thank you*, went against everything
in your gut. Even so, the attendant leaned all her weight
on thin pale arms, reached her head out the window
of the guard booth and glanced down at your left arm,
bound and supported with leather straps from the web
of your hand to just below the elbow, the middle and ring fingers
held loosely with Velcro, while your right arm, lean with muscle
extended, holding out the full price of admission for one car.

She should see you peel an orange. Such precision.
With one hand and a sharp knife, you gracefully orbit the bright peel,
seem barely to touch it. After putting down the knife,
your thumb nudges the top—just under the imprint of the stem—
and the peel falls away, a curved slide, like an Escher print,
only seconds later to lie seamlessly back in shape,
sitting on the table as if it had just fallen from the tree.

# Full Again

She never thinks to wear a hat.
On her walk to the grape fields,
she sees those other women,
light faces shaded in tightly woven hats,
pruning their rose bushes in khaki culottes.
What a beautiful species, she thinks,
when they dab their glowing foreheads
with embroidered handkerchiefs.

Behind the long, straight rows,
she reaches and picks and pulls
and sorts until the lissome dusk
descends. Her solid arms strain to grab,
stoop low to swoop. Her eyes peer deeply
into the vines for the grapes'
small roundness. She builds crates
and folds boxes, hefts bushels
onto the beds of trucks.
All day she works.

In the quiet of evening, the heavy
denim pants, stained t-shirt,
and ripped, long-sleeved flannel, lie
like a shell of herself on the bathroom floor.
She can just be female now:
damp from the shower, breasts
resting flat to either side, fingers

splayed wide like fawn-lily petals
against her soft stomach.

# Working with Paul, Irene's Café

He cooks like he's my wife,
this large, paroled Border Brother
with tattoos of busty gyrating women
and the Aztec sun blanketing his arms
wrists to elbows. He brings me a plate,
tells me to eat it and don't ask
questions—the plate is steaming
with vegetables sautéed in garlic butter,
basil-crusted salmon, peppered potatoes.

It's too much food for me
while on shift, but I'm sitting
in one of the vinyl, palm-tree-decorated
booths, and he's standing over me
like a warden, or maybe
like my grandmother, his apron stained,
his shoes shiny with grease,
beads of sweat over his top lip.
I smile. *It looks good, I guess.*
I tell him this, teasing, pulling
on the dark rope of his braid that swings
longer than the base of his spine.

He smiles back, and I can see
what his mama must see
in those bright, obsidian eyes.
I take a bite and taste the time

he spent chopping basil,
walking through the farmer's market
pinching squash, wondering
whether or not I would like it.
*It's not bad*, I tell him. *Not bad at all.*

## Grandma's Hands
*For Lupe Chavez*

If one were not looking closely,
it might appear she was making
a half-hearted fist, forgetting
to pull down the forefinger and pinkie
and tuck in the thumb—

but upon closer inspection, one would see
that was all that was left
of those fingers—the skin just above
the knuckle folded in on itself
like the husk of a tamale.

As a child I would touch her
gaudy rings—their costume gems
big enough to consume
those half fingers—
just to feel
the soft tops
of her hands, so unlike
her palms, calloused
from pruning pomegranate
and orange trees.
I imagined the many ways
she could have lost
the tops of two fingers—
in a cannery accident perhaps,

the teeth of a machine no longer content
with the taste of aluminum and steel.

Or maybe it happened
when she was a young girl
in Mexico City playing among
the shootings, kidnappings,
and bad cóyotes—
why we never went to visit.

What if she was merely tired
of this life she was born into and wanted
to stop it all. The struggle of being
a wife and mother and worker and woman
here is back-breaking.
*Nah, that's only how gabachos*
*with no work ethic think,* my uncle says.

I think then of her smile,
the one that would come
with the first light of morning
on the days when my sister and I would sleep
overnight on the living room floor
across from the statue of La Virgen de Guadalupe
where we were allowed to lay roses.
She would gently wipe
the sleep from my eyes
with one of her whole fingers,
lay open her palms before me.
I'd lay my right hand in her

right hand and my left in her left,
her strength enough for both of us.

# Praise this Land, The San Joaquin Valley

Praise this land whose arms opened to the sky's lost children.
Praise to the rotating tires along the asphalt laid by these children
and their children's children, a rainbow of children whose hair
is long and straight, whose hair is short and kinky, whose hair is red
like the strawberries at the roadside stand.

Praise to the roadside stand and the dark man sweating under a colorful umbrella,
and the fleece blankets for sale hung across a taut-drawn line,
their designs of cats and football emblems, roses and the Virgin Mother
with her hands outstretched to Diego illuminating culture from across the freeway.
Praise industry and hard work, calloused hands and squinted eyes.
Praise remittances and work sheds, green onions and tomatoes.

Praise your ancestors who loved the land like their own flesh
and massaged its parched roughness with water and rancheras, whose tan
fingers sank deep into the soil to make holes into which they whispered
*La tierra, te alabo*. Praise the generations who sang to the Earth,

whose songs were carried by the winds and scattered like seeds
that were planted and grew more songs and more songs, until the plunge
of the hoe between rows of cilantro released thousands of loving voices
whose words say *Praise me, praise me, you made me.*

# V

"come celebrate
with me that everyday
something has tried to kill me
and has failed."
                    - Lucille Clifton

# Earth Day—Fresno, CA 2002
### for Christy


I miss the Earth Days on the Fresno County Courthouse yard,
where the bust of Martin Luther King Jr. looked out
approvingly over the tables of vegan home-baked
muffins, seitan burgers, and fruit fresh from the trees
that surround the city like the hem of a great and generous skirt.

We wore tie-dyed tank tops and ripped jeans, hugged
the thin textured bark of the hybrid poplars, and danced
wildly, barefoot on the lush irrigated grass to bands wearing
the colors of their indigenous tribes, who swayed rhythmically
to the sounds of their maracas, cow-hide drums and acoustic guitars.

It was the only day everyone was relaxed in front of that monstrous
building, constructed like a thick wall, winking suspiciously
with the aid of afternoon sun. The hippies, conservationists,
policemen, lawyers, defense attorneys, homeless schizophrenics, released
prostitutes, and college students all gathered together this day,

euphorically drinking filtered rain water and lemonade, loving trees
and clean air, forgetting—if only until the rise of the moon—
that we were all trying to stake out an individual space, dividing
the city grid between have and have not.

# On a Summer Afternoon

Long-haired William in his ripped jeans tells me
the body is made of millions upon millions of moving
particles, molecules, and that if it weren't for gravity,
they would release like helium balloons from a net.

He places his hand on my thigh and asks if I can feel
my molecules moving against his. Can I feel them
blending and trading, gravity working like a conductor
where our skins connect? My body begins to feel

ethereal as we sit on the porch, afternoon light
shining in blades between the spindles of the railing.
I think I like the idea of our molecules combining—
first hand to thigh, then hand to face, then chests
and legs. Foreheads and noses, eyes and lips.

I imagine that, like pointillist paintings, from a distance
our fragments together must look plenary, sublime.

# Working with Tyrell at Uncle Harry's Bagels

He was always in his baker's uniform:
black pants, black Adidas, white jacket,
rows of buttons spaced four deep across

the breast. After work, he'd take the jacket off
and sit out front on the patio in his stained
undershirt, smoking and drinking Dr. Pepper

from a clear plastic cup he stole from the supply closet.
At the Christmas party in 2001, after a twelve-
hour shift, we locked the glass double doors

and all the baristas, cashiers, and shift leaders
exchanged gag gifts. He and Jesse chipped in
and bought me a lacy, pink-trimmed

Victoria Secret camisole and matching thong.
*Hold it up, girl. Hold it up for everyone to see*,
Tyrell shouted when I looked up, confused,

from the contents of the meticulously wrapped
box, its gold satin bow drooping unevenly.
*We sold extra mota to the richies at Jamba Juice*

*to afford that*, Jesse said, winking. *That means you gotta*
*at least try it on for us*. And that's how things were
in our world, serving bagels to defense attorneys

and heart surgeons, extra hot lattes to rich, old biddies
and the owner's steroid-juiced friends who always
wanted extra cream cheese, extra lox, extra time

on the patio with the most fresh-faced girl behind
the counter. We "accidentally" dropped their bagels
face down on the high-trafficked floor, went in the back

while customers waited, and leaned into each other,
my cheek resting between the broad-set shoulder
blades of Tyrell's back, my nostrils filling with

the scent of garlic and yeast. Between rushes,
we crammed into the walk-in and lit up, blowing
fragrant smoke into one another's mouths to conserve
what little we had for ourselves.

# My First Tattoo

The spring after we turn 18, my friend Liz and I
walk the four miles south from Memorial High in the heat
of Central Valley's late May, cars buzzing down Blackstone, hand
in hand toward the parlor where we'd decided to get our tattoos.
The artist's name was Turtle. Her body was small and tight, skin
dark like an indio, like Alma's before she got sent back.

While we count out our cash, Liz says, *There's no going back
now* and smiles, expecting me to be afraid, to talk myself out of it, like I
do sometimes with things I want. Like the time we laid out, skin
against skin, naked in the privacy of her backyard, the heat
from the sun reddening her lower back, where the tattoo
of *Le Chat Noir* she chose will go. Turtle washes her hands

before pulling latex gloves over her blunt fingers. Liz hands
me her purse. *I'll go first*, she says, going around the counter, sitting back-
wards on the worn-looking adjustable hospital stool. *Your tattoo*,
Turtle asks circling a finger at the base of Liz's spine, *you want it here?* I
see Liz nod, brace herself at the buzz of the needle that sounds like heat
that escapes with steam. I watch the color slip brightly under her white skin,

the needle oscillating, alive. It's funny how you have to break the skin,
shatter through to the dermis beneath to make the color last. Turtle's hands
don't look like hands that damage, that break and scar. I can feel heat
radiating off her body even from across the glass counter. Her lower back
is exposed, the elastic of boxers beneath her jeans. Her skin, I
think, looks like the finely ground cocoa Abuela puts in her coffee. *Tattoos*,

79

Turtle says without looking up, *were a sign of courage for the Mayans. Tattoos*
*were offerings to the Aztec gods and placement was sacred. Our skin*
*the most divine gift we could give.* She wipes the blood from Liz's back. I
know I am next. Liz's eyes brim with tears, her face flush with pain. I hand
her a Kleenex from my pocket and press my lips to her cheek. My back
is where I want it. Same as Liz. I am not afraid of the heat

that pain produces. Its diffusion around trauma is comforting. Heat
has always accompanied me, engulfing my body like an aura. This tattoo
will be no different. I want it so bad my stomach turns. My back
tingles where Turtle rubs the alcohol, where she presses the design transfer. My skin
is hers now. I am surrendered to this beautiful boyish woman, her hands
the only things I think about, the only things I can picture. I

long for the heat she'll create that will spread over all my skin—
this tattoo proof that she touched me, that her hands
and my back were courageous, worked in harmony: she, the tattoo, and I.

# Neighborhood Watch

This neighborhood really is like the TV show *227* with all the ladies sitting on the brownstone steps watching the dark-skinned children play double-dutch in the street and gossiping about the midnight love songs of the couple in apartment B or the attractive single man living on the third floor. But we're not in a brownstone. Our two-level complex opens like a U. We sit under the shade of a fruiting orange tree in thrift-store lawn chairs, smoke Chesterfields and drink Pepsi or sometimes, on payday, Negra Modelos, and wait for the mother whose husband killed himself four months after their baby was born (he was dead in the apartment for seventeen hours before she called the police). We help her with her groceries. We wait for Andrew in apartment C who lost his construction job five months ago, who in the daytime drinks with his buddies in the house frames they built, bare as stripped bone. The men sit in the gaping window holes, throwing their beer cans out onto the ground that would have been someone's lawn. You can never tell what mood he'll be in when he comes home. We don't want to wait until it is painted onto the cheeks of his girlfriend. When we go inside for the night, the low pulse of reggae from the bar and the steady drum of traffic are a lullaby. We keep a couple windows open just in case.

# Another Epistle

## I.

Dear Carole, you never told me
silence could be so satisfying.
The other day, I almost told
another stranger to fuck off.
It took all I had to look
through the filmy windshield
of her boxy Fiat
and lock eyes with her.
She pretended not to see me
going through the crosswalk
as she Cali-rolled
six inches from my legs.
But my stare—
smart as a slap—
made her look.
*I arrest you with my gaze,*
I said in my head as she
tried not to look back.
My eyes did not release her
until I had both
feet on the sidewalk.

## II.

You did tell me words

were dangerous.
Not words themselves, mind you
(signifier and signified
and all that shit, not that you
or I knew that then),
but you knew the words themselves
meant nothing
until they reached the ears
of another person.
Like the time we were walking
home from Six Star Factory Outlet
and that guy leaned
his balding head out the window
to whistle and I told him he could
shove that whistle up his ass.
He chased us
in his beat-up Bonneville,
driving through the parking lot
until we got to a chain-link fence
with a hole. I grappled,
hand over hand, feet
skimming the steel,
while you tried to squeeze
through the rift
between chain and post,
getting stuck. From the other side,
I laughed, and it was the power
of that laugh that pulled you through.
I couldn't believe
the way the ragged chain-links

clawed at your curvy hips,
caught at the button
on your jeans.
*Like Winnie the Pooh at Rabbit's,*
I kept repeating.
It didn't hurt
when you slapped me
on the arm the next day,
but I stopped saying it anyhow.
For your lazy ass
to put down a cigarette
and attempt to inflict harm,
it must've really pissed you off.

III.

Today, I counted
the number of people taking
the bus 'cause they had to,
versus the Keen-wearing,
granola types trying to reduce
their carbon footprint.
I wish you'd lived long enough
to take the bus
to save Mother Earth.
Not that you would have.
You'd probably drive
a Cadillac that twinkled
pink in the sun,
one with hypnotic hub caps.

I'd probably be ashamed
to know you. I'd be standing
at the bus stop next to some
hipster with a fixie
and one of those BPA-free
stainless-steel water bottles.
We'd see your Caddy speeding
down Blackstone,
and that hipster would say,
*What kind of woman drives a car like that?*
I'd nod, say, *Some kind of new-money pimp.*
You just liked to be surrounded
by beautiful things—
at least that's what you'd say
as you tucked
a stray hair behind my ear
with your soft, white hand.
*Beautiful things.*

## Cheers to the Dead

I wonder if he's hungry,
there in his grave among
the sediment and microorganisms.

The Hmong relatives of his neighbors
bring bowls of rice and vegetables,
sweet dishes whose names I can't
pronounce, and cans of Coke.
All he gets are American flags
and flowers.

Even in death,
they won't let Grandpa eat or drink.
He loved to tell me how
Grandma kept him to one beer
a day after the doctor told them
it was colon cancer,
and on that first Sunday my dad
brought two forties of Old English,
one for each of them.
*You said one beer, Toni.*

I imagine the looks on their faces,
how they must have sat
in lawn chairs in the shade, grilling
boneless chicken breasts, raising
their heavy, sweating bottles

to Grandma as she gazed down
from the kitchen window, her eyes
narrow, lips tight.

So, I travel with two six-packs
of Anchor Steam in the middle of the night
when the round light of the moon
is all that guides my way through
the cemetery. I grope to find
his headstone, the name and dates
etched in the marble
as in memory, and crack the cap
on each bottle, pouring
one six-pack onto the freshly mowed grass
above his body, saving
the other for myself.

I sit against a tree, and we
discuss what will happen
when my mother and grandmother
come by in the morning
after church, with their cloying lilacs
and mini, Dollar Store flags.
We laugh to think of my mom kneeling
to place the flowers in the built-in vase,
discovering the ground soaked.
What we wouldn't give to see
the looks on their faces as they drive home,
somber and perfumed with hops.

# My Own Song
*after N. Scott Momaday*

I am a leaf gliding on the light breeze
I am the squirrel that jumps across trees
I am the koi that leaps, shining in the courthouse pond
I am the shadow of a streetlight
I am the signal's yellow circle, the red of the stop sign
I am a junkie joking near the dumpster
I am the pocketful of stolen rosaries
I am the roaming helicopter overhead
I am the warm light of sunset
I am the roaring of the low riders
I am the glitter of broken glass beneath your window
I am the long track of a needle
I am the flame of a lighter
I am a stray dog sidling away in the dusk
I am a field of tent city shacks and the community garden
I am an angel dangling from the rearview mirror
I am the empty stomach of a young child
I am the whole dream of these things

You see, I am alive, I am alive
I stand in good relation to the city
I stand in good relation to the cops
I stand in good relation to all that is dark and lovely
I stand in good relation to the daughters of industry
You see, I am alive, I am alive

# El Traspatio de mi Abuela

— *If we were to subject the topic of the sacredness of lands to a Western rational analysis, fully recognizing that such an analysis is merely for our convenience in discussion and does not represent the nature of reality, we would probably find four major categories of description: 1. A site within our own history, regardless of group, something of great importance took place, 2.&3. Lands where holy revelations have been revealed, 4. Openness to new revelations in new spaces.*
—Vine Deloria Jr. from "Sacred Lands and Religious Freedom"


My abuela's yard may not look like
a sacred place, but it meets
the four major categories
of sacred description.
This is convenient.
In her yard, there are four corners
that point
to the four directions.
In each of these directions,
guardians stand:
to the north, faces La Virgen de Guadalupe,
to the south Saint Francis of Assisi
while Coatlicue stares to the west,
and Eagle east.


1.
Forget that her yard
is in Merced, which is in the Central Valley,
in California, which once belonged
to Mexico, which once belonged
to the indigenous tribes. To get from those
tribes to the present day city of Merced,

a name that means favor or mercy, there had to be
a whole lot of merciless favors.

If you put your ear to the dirt, you can hear
the blood cries push through
the cracks in the crusted Earth.
It was in this yard, in 2002
where I caught my abuelo
sneaking a smoke behind the nectarine tree.
He bought my silence with a cigarette.
We breathed quietly, each holding
the inevitable in our lungs,
the birth of our inside joke,
our relationship, where he remained grandfather
and I granddaughter, standing
beside the pink rose bushes.

2.
Like Joshua's triumph,
hauling that heavy Ark of the Covenant
across land that should have been water,
this yard became water
when it should have been land.
The whole neighborhood prayed
in that deep month of drought
for God's mercy on their crops.
My grandmother, loudest of all, kissed la Virgen's feet
and crossed herself multiple times a day
until the mighty Goodness
broke a water main

at the corner of V Street and Emory.
The treated city water flowed
into the yards like the Euphrates—
or maybe El Rio Grande.
My grandmother planted kisses
on her four guardians and erected a bird-bath
where the water had begun to flow under the fence
as a marker, so that when her grandchildren
ask their father in time,
*What mean she by this bird-bath?*
He shall answer.


3.
From the roots of all its plants,
this yard teems with religiosity.
These plants talk, using a voice from the gods
to instruct us in the ways of survival.
The cactus raised in his clay pot
beckons and tells us to call him Nopales.
He details the cutting of his arms,
the removal of spines,
his delicious usefulness in omelets and salads.


The cilantro whispers seductively,
the green onions sing us psalms,
the spinach recites ancient verse,
and we thank them and honor
those who speak to us
by replanting.

4.
After all, it is a yard with common grass,
where family dogs shit and Uncle George
taught me to shoot a crossbow
using a stuffed bunny for a target.
A yard, only 40 years a yard,
exposed as sacred through revelation
on a normal day, when sunlight trickled quietly
through the leaves of the trees
and we went out to pick nectarines.

I climbed the ladder, reached out my arm,
placed my fingers on the fruit's smooth skin,
twisted it away from the stem,
and handed it down to my grandmother,
whose hair danced lightly in the breeze.
*Esta tierra es buena para nosotros, mija,* she said,
her face shining like an altar candle.

# GLOSSARY OF SPANISH WORDS AND PHRASES

*Está tan caliente* —it's so hot

*baile folklorico* —folk dancing

*zapateadas* —dance shoes, specifically for the traditional folk dances of Mexico and Spain

*Esto es usted* —this is you

*y usted debería estar orgulloso* —and you should be proud

*hermanas* —sisters

*mota* —slang term for marijuana

*Telemundo* —Spanish-language television channel

*chile verde* —green chile

*Imperio De Cristal* —Crystal Empire (a soap opera)

*Beso, abrazo, amor* and *familia* —kiss, hug, love, and family

*Quinceañera* —a celebration; a rite of passage from girlhood to womanhood; a coming-of-age ritual marking when a girl has her fifteenth birthday, similar to a European debutante ball

*Practique para luego* —to practice

*Mija* —affectionate slang conjunction of *mi hija*, meaning my daughter or my girl

*cóyotes* —a colloquial Mexican-Spanish term for people who smuggle undocumented migrants over the U.S.-Mexico border

*gabachos* —originally meaning literally a foreigner or outsider, but colloquially it has become a Chicano pejorative term for English-speaking, non-Latino (non-Hispanic) people

*La tierra, te alabo* —Earth, I praise you

*Coatlicue* —Nahuatl (ancient Aztec language) meaning "The Mother of Gods"; Coatlicue is the goddess who gave birth to the moon, stars, and sun

*Esta tierra es buena para nosotros, mija* —the land is good to us, my daughter

# GRACIAS

I want to extend special thanks to my teachers, mentors, friends, and fellow writers without whom these poems would have left the confines of my computer. Many thanks to the Department of English at the University of Nebraska-Lincoln, specifically my dissertation committee chair Grace Bauer and the dissertation committee members, Amelia Montes and Joy Castro. Your guidance, support, revision suggestions, and modeling what it looks like to be a strong and successful teacher/scholar/writer were invaluable. Thank you to my poetry peers and friends Cody Lumpkin, Jennifer Case, James Crews, and Hali Sofala for out-of-class shop talk over many coffees, meals, and then miles; you have seen these poems almost as much I have. To Wendy Oleson and Clarence Harlan Orsi for after-hours community and crafts. Thanks also to my colleagues at Marshall University who have been immensely supportive of my creative work and travels.

An extra special thank you to the editors at Sundress Publications for this amazing opportunity and supportive dedication to the written word, and especially to Erin Elizabeth Smith, for her keen editing suggestions on this manuscript and for inviting me to be part of every step of the process.

Thank you to the amazingly talented artist Aydee Lopez Martinez for the generous use of her resonant painting, "Self Love," for the cover.

An extra-special thank you to my familia: Mom, for your encouragement to be outspoken and honest; Dad, for your unwavering example of strength and work ethnic; mi hermana, Christy, for being my life-long partner in crime. All my grandparents/abuelitos, for your love and stories.

And a double extra-special thank you to Daniel Lewis whose love and support is vast and multifaceted. This journey could not have happened without you.

# ABOUT THE AUTHOR

Sarah A. Chavez, a mestiza born and raised in the California Central Valley, is the author of the chapbook, *All Day, Talking* (dancing girl press, 2014), a selection of which won the Susan Atefat Peckham Fellowship (2013). In 2016, she was listed as one of the Top Ten "New" Latino Authors to Watch (and Read) by LatinoStories.com and her poetry has been nominated for *Best New Poets 2015* and *Best of the Net 2016*. Her work has appeared in anthologies such as *Imaniman: Poets Writing in the Anzaldúan Borderlands* (Aunt Lute Books) and *Political Punch: Contemporary Poems on the Politics of Identity* (Sundress Publications), as well as the journals *Brevity*, *North American Review*, *Fourth River*, *Acentos Review*, and *VIDA Exclusive*, among others. Chavez holds a PhD in English with a focus in poetry and Ethnic Studies from the University of Nebraska-Lincoln. She is currently a Visiting Assistant Professor teaching Ethnic American literature and creative writing at Marshall University where she also serves as the coordinator of the A.E. Stringer Visiting Writers Series.

# OTHER SUNDRESS TITLES

*They Were Bears*
Sarah Marcus
$15

*Posada: Offerings of Witness and Refuge*
Xochitl Julisa Bermejo
$15

*Theater of Parts*
M. Mack
$15

*Every Love Story is an Apocalypse Story*
Donna Vorreyer
$14

*major characters in minor films*
Kristy Bowen
$14

*Fortress*
Kristina Marie Darling
$14

*The Hardship Post*
Jehanne Dubrow
$14

*The Bone Folders*
T.A. Noonan
$14

*Big Thicket Blues*
Natalie Giarratano
$15

*At Whatever Front*
Les Kay
$15

*Suites for the Modern Dancer*
Jill Khoury
$15

*Ha Ha Ha Thump*
Amorak Huey
$14

*Confluence*
Sandra Marchetti
$14

*When I Wake It Will Be Forever*
Virginia Smith Rice
$14

*One Perfect Bird*
Letitia Trent
$14

*Babbage's Dream*
Neil Aitken
$15

*No More Milk*
Karen Craigo
$15

*What Will Keep Us Alive*
Kristin LaTour
$14

*Stationed Near the Gateway*
Margaret Bashaar
$14

*Hallelujah for the Ghosties*
Melanie Jordan
$14

*Virginia Smith Rice*
Donna Vorreyer
$14

*Like a Fish*
Daniel Crocker
$14

CPSIA information can be obtained
at www.ICGtesting.com
Printed in the USA
FSOW02n1146090917
38535FS